HOW TO CRAFT A
CEO BRAND
ON LINKEDIN

2023 EDITION

CREATE A POWERFUL PERSONAL BRAND,
BUILD YOUR AUDIENCE & GET THE VISIBILITY YOU DESERVE

JUDY SCHRAMM

Table of Contents

7   **ChatGPT & LinkedIn**

Chapter 1

Why Your Personal Brand Matters

When you build a strong personal brand, you attract the people who believe what you believe, want what you want, and can help you get there faster.

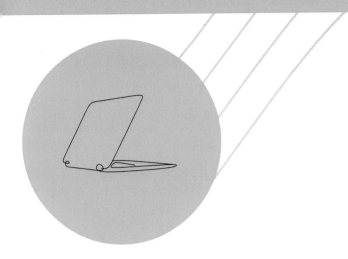

Over the years, throughout your career, you have built a strong personal brand. That brand has been a critical part of your success. People have chosen to do business with you, invest in you, hire you, work for you, partner with you — all because of who you are.

But how visible is your brand online? If you are like many CEOs, your brand only reaches people who know you personally. That limits your ability to make an impact.

To maximize your personal leverage and give your business the greatest advantage, it is essential to make your brand visible online. You need to craft your brand authentically, so it reflects who you are and delivers the information you want people to have about you.

When you do that effectively, you attract the right people and get them excited about doing business with you.

This book is about how to build your brand on LinkedIn

LinkedIn has become your professional presence online.

Google yourself, and your LinkedIn profile is likely one of the first search results. Use Microsoft 365? The LinkedIn profiles of people who email you are a click away. Both Google and Microsoft are driving people to your LinkedIn profile.

Take advantage of this!

Use LinkedIn to feed people the exact information you want them to have about you. Share your story, advocate for your solutions, and promote your company culture.

In this book, we show you how to put LinkedIn to work for you to create a personal presence that impresses people, educates them, and gets them excited about engaging with you.

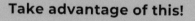

Our focus is on strategy – what to do, rather than how to do it.

We haven't included how-to screenshots, in part because LinkedIn is so intuitive, we don't think they are needed. But it's also because LinkedIn changes constantly, so any screenshots and instructions would be out of date quickly. If you need to learn how to do something, just do a quick search on Google or YouTube.

We did include a chapter on how to use ChatGPT to make building your brand easier. AI tool capabilities are evolving rapidly and likely will have changed by the time you read this, but we felt it was important to include because AI makes writing so much faster!

If you want help with any of this, connect with me or one of my team members on LinkedIn. We answer simple questions for free.

Should you want more advice, you can get an hour with one of our LinkedIn coaches. You can also have us write your LinkedIn profile or design your personal LinkedIn strategy.

You can participate in webinars and LinkedIn Lives every month.

See current and archived events at:
www.proresource.com/webinars.

Please do join us!

We want you to love LinkedIn as much as we do.

Judy Schramm, CEO
ProResource, Inc.

March 2023

Chapter 2

LinkedIn Profile Essentials

Use your LinkedIn profile to make people feel like they know you, like you, and can trust you.

When someone googles you, your LinkedIn profile is probably the #1 or #2 search result.

This is your opportunity to give people the exact information you want them to discover — to impress them, build trust, and create opportunities to engage.

Of all the people who google you, there are some who are more relevant to you than others. Perhaps you are focused on lead generation and prospects matter most to you. Or you are in hiring mode and care more about prospective employees. Or you are raising a round and focusing on investors.

Who do you care about most?

Write your profile for those people.

Once upon a time, LinkedIn was a resumé database. It isn't just resumés anymore. If you are looking for a new job, by all means, write your profile to attract recruiters. But if you are doing lead generation, write to customers. If you are hiring, write to prospective employees.

Later in the book, we discuss tailoring your profile to specific objectives. Here, we'll talk more generally and share best practices.

Profile Photo

LinkedIn says profiles with a photo receive 14x more views. But don't just upload a casual photo. Use a professional headshot – it's worth the investment. In our own experiments, a higher quality photo increased profile views by 32%.

We recommend using a photographer who specializes in social media headshots. A good photographer will light you so you look younger and slimmer, but more importantly, they will capture your personality so your brand comes through in a powerful way.

Header Graphic

One of the easiest and most impactful changes you can make to your profile is to add a header image behind your profile photo. Choose a strong graphic that makes a statement about your personal brand.

Here are some good options:

- For corporate branding, use your logo or an image from the home page of your website.

- For lead generation, use a photo that shows your product or the type of customers you work with.

- To promote company culture, use a photo of your team.

- To demonstrate authority, use a photo of a speaking engagement, your book, or a TV appearance.

- To highlight your location, use a cityscape or photo of a well-known landmark.

Make sure you own the photo or have permission to use it. The current ideal image size is 1584 x 396 pixels (4:1 ratio). Use a jpg or png, and keep the file size under 8MB.

Note: LinkedIn's user interface is responsive, which means your header graphic will display differently depending on the device used to view the profile. You can't fully control the placement of your logo and any text. We recommend putting logos and text at the top of the image or on the right.

Headline

Your headline is the line that appears immediately below your name at the top of your profile. By default, LinkedIn populates the headline with your current job title and company. But don't use the default.

Use your headline to tell people who you help and how you can help them. Make it keyword-rich and compelling.

Your headline can have up to 120 characters, including spaces. (If you edit on your phone, you may get up to 220 characters.) Put the most important information at the beginning, since in some places the headline will be truncated.

Use | or * or a comma to separate concepts and make your headline more readable. Some people use emojis or wingdings, but while they make your title stand out, they can look spammy.

Need Examples?

You can find lists of excellent CEO LinkedIn profiles on our website: *www.proresource.com/excellent-linkedin-ceo-profiles*

About

Your About section functions like a cover letter for your LinkedIn profile. This is the best place to tell your story.

Share your why.
If you are a founder, include why you started the business.

Share your mission.
Why does what you do have meaning to you?

Share your vision.
What are you working towards?

Share your who.
Who do you work with? How do you help them?

Share your traction.
What milestones have you achieved? What are you most proud of?

The first four lines are critical. For people to read the rest, they have to click on "see more." So grab their attention early and get them interested. We like to begin with a story, which is the most effective way to draw people in. But a quotation or unusual statement will also work.

Speak in the language of your audience. Feel free to use industry buzzwords if your goal is to connect with educated prospects and demonstrate your expertise. If the people you are targeting won't necessarily recognize those terms, stick with plain business language so everyone can understand your value proposition.

Give people a sense of your personality, and feel free to let them see your passion for what you do. You'll attract others who feel the same way.

The current trend is towards shorter summaries. But you have 2,000 characters to work with, which is 285-500 words. Take as much space as you need to tell your story — people will read it all when you make it interesting.

About Section Tips

1. Write in the first person.
2. Tell a story.
3. Incorporate keywords.

Featured

This relatively new section of the LinkedIn profile provides a place where you can upload or link to articles, blog posts, videos, podcasts, presentations, images, and documents. Include:

> Press coverage — recent or impressive articles about your company

> Podcasts or video interviews

> Awards

> Recent blog posts

Use this section to build credibility, showcase your speaking skills, and provide opportunities for people to learn more.

Experience

In this section, share how you acquired your expertise.

You probably already have your job titles, companies, and dates filled in. Now add the details. Here is what you should include for each job:

- Unless the company is a household name, start with a sentence or two that explains what the business does. Not sure what to say? Go to the company's website and look at the About page.

- What was your role? What were your responsibilities?

- What were your accomplishments? What are you proud of?

- What did you learn that contributed to what you are doing now?

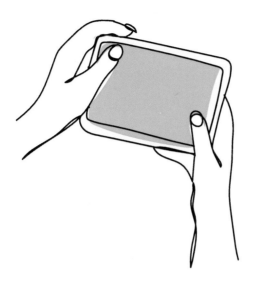

You can also upload or link to videos, presentations, documents, and images for each job. They will not have the same prominence as adding them to the Featured section, but they add richness to your profile.

If you are on a board, you can include that role here instead of in the Volunteer section. Just drag and drop it below your primary role.

Are Company Logos Visible for Each Job?

If not, you need to connect to the LinkedIn page for that business. Click on the pencil icon to edit the company name. Start typing, and LinkedIn will bring up a list of companies. Select the correct one and save. You should now see the logo.

Contact Info

You can include three links to websites and blogs. Link to your company website and blog first. Then think about other online resources people will find valuable — maybe a landing page or your jobs page? Or include a link to your calendar so people can easily schedule a call.

If you want people to contact you, include a work email.

You can also add Twitter, WhatsApp, Skype, WeChat, and other ways to reach you.

SEO Tip

Incoming links from LinkedIn can give your company's search engine visibility a boost, so make sure your whole team uses those links.

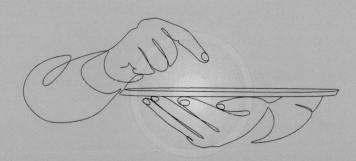

Personalized URL

LinkedIn allows you to personalize the URL of your profile. We recommend doing this, as it makes the URL easier to remember and share.

Name Pronunciation

If your name is often mispronounced, record your preferred pronunciation.

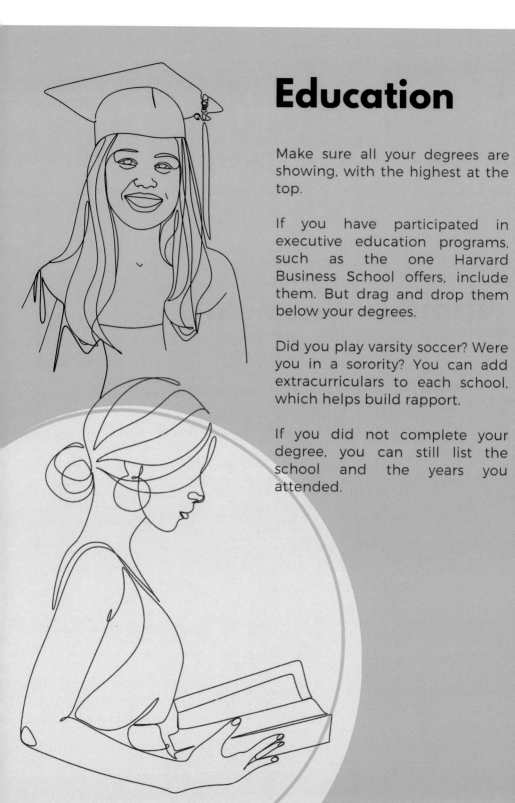

Education

Make sure all your degrees are showing, with the highest at the top.

If you have participated in executive education programs, such as the one Harvard Business School offers, include them. But drag and drop them below your degrees.

Did you play varsity soccer? Were you in a sorority? You can add extracurriculars to each school, which helps build rapport.

If you did not complete your degree, you can still list the school and the years you attended.

Gender Pronouns

Show your support for diversity by adding gender pronouns to your profile.

Volunteer Experience & Causes

Volunteering shows you care about your community and believe in giving back.

When you add an association, non-profit, or cause to your profile, you promote that organization and spread the word about their mission.

Skills & Endorsements

You can include up to 50 skills. You can choose the top three, which will be visible on your profile. The others can be found after clicking "Show all skills."

LinkedIn has more than 40,000 skills included in its database. Simply start typing and LinkedIn will auto-complete, suggesting up to 10 options.

LinkedIn is currently categorizing skills into four groups:

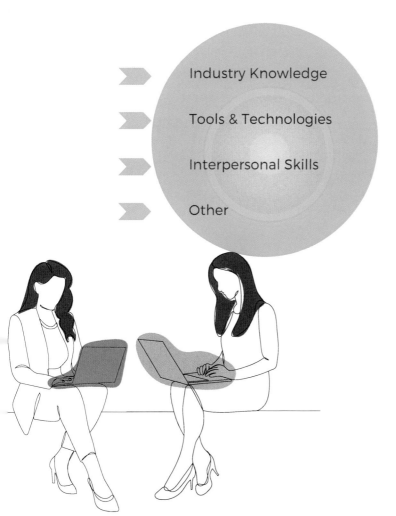

Industry Knowledge

Tools & Technologies

Interpersonal Skills

Other

For a well-rounded portfolio of skills, include these types:

Products/services your company offers

Industries you serve

Technology: AI, IoT, Blockchain

Business issues: DEI, ESG

Certifications: Six Sigma, CISSP

Technical skills: software languages, platforms, tools

Management skills: leadership, strategy, turnarounds, IPO

Recommendations

Recommendations on LinkedIn are short statements from connections who have worked with you. They are useful because people who visit your profile can see who has endorsed you and what they said about your work.

The simplest way to get recommendations is to give recommendations. Write them for the people whose recommendations you'd like. Most will return the favor.

Another way to get recommendations is to draft them yourself. You can request a recommendation and say "I was hoping you could say something like this…"

This makes it much easier for the person you are asking, because they don't have to figure out what to say — they can simply modify your suggestion.

Get recommendations from a variety of people, such as customers, direct reports, partners, and peers.

More Sections

The LinkedIn profile includes more than 10 other sections to help you tell your story and add richness to your profile. They give you an opportunity to show your range, highlight awards, and include quirky details.

Sections include:

- Certifications
- Honors & Awards
- Languages
- Patents
- Projects
- Publications
- Organizations

Put articles, books, ebooks, and podcasts in Publications. You can include quality articles written by you, about you, or about your business.

Projects is a useful section where you can include mini case studies or highlight particularly interesting projects where you played a key role.

Final Tips

Proof your profile, looking for spelling, grammar, and formatting errors. Typos make your profile look sloppy.

Incorporate keywords. What phrases would someone search on if they were looking for someone like you? Include those in your profile. The most important places to put keywords are your headline, About section, Experience, and Skills.

Don't let your profile get stale. Update quarterly with new videos, articles, and accomplishments. Changing your header graphic is also a good way to keep your profile fresh.

Chapter 3

Your Network

Fill your network with people you want paying attention to you.

Now that you have a strong LinkedIn profile, the next step is to build your network.

The magic number in LinkedIn is 500 connections. A CEO should usually have at least 2,000. You have more stakeholders than anyone else in your company, and there's value in building connections and relationships with all of them.

However, focus on quality more than quantity. The people who view your profile can see the connections you have in common. When those are people they respect and trust, you go up in their estimation.

Make it your goal to fill your network with people you care about, where the relationship has meaning to you.

Build Your Network Strategically

There are three types of people you will want to connect with:

- People you want to stay in touch with

- People you want to do business with

- People who are connected to and respected by your audience

The first group is straightforward. When you meet someone interesting and have a good conversation, invite them to connect.

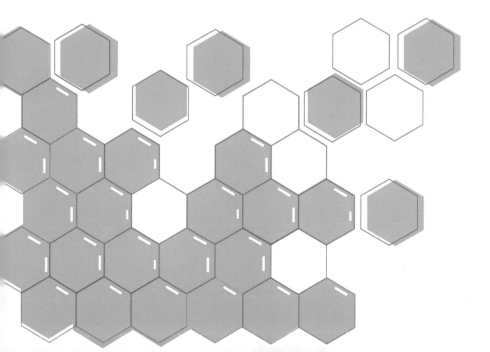

With the second group, be proactive. LinkedIn is the perfect place to identify people who would make good customers, partners, or employees and introduce yourself. Once connected, you have permission to stay in touch with them — and they will keep their own contact information up to date for you.

The third group matters because LinkedIn shows people what connections you have in common. If visitors see that you are connected to people they know and respect, you gain instant credibility.

Who should you be connected to? Here's a short list:

Customers

Customers are some of your best connections. But don't just connect with your primary contact.

Here's why:

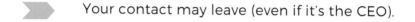 Your contact may leave (even if it's the CEO).

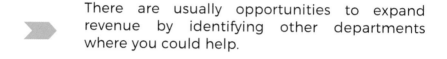 There are usually opportunities to expand revenue by identifying other departments where you could help.

The more people you are connected to in an organization, the more credibility you have when you invite someone else to connect. For example, if you are connected to 30 people at IBM, that's much more impressive than just two or three.

The more people you are connected to, the more insight you have into what's going on at the company. LinkedIn notifies you when people get promoted or change jobs, which can be very useful.

Prospects

Anytime you talk to a prospect — over the phone, on a webinar, or through email — take the opportunity to connect on LinkedIn.

Suspects

These are people you want to work with but haven't yet met. Prepare to introduce yourself to a decision-maker by connecting with others in the company. Look for employees with whom you can connect quickly, typically those who have a premium version of LinkedIn or a large network. Make enough connections and you will more easily reach the decision-makers.

Referrers

These are people who can refer business to you. They might have products or services that complement your solutions, work with smaller businesses or larger accounts, or work in a nearby region.

Most people will accept an invitation to connect that says "It looks like we work with similar types of customers. Could we set up a call so I can learn more about your business and your ideal clients? I'd like to be able to refer people to you."

Employees

Connect with your employees. It will give you insights into what they are thinking, and you'll learn from seeing how they use LinkedIn.

Vendors

Vendors are connected with many people in an industry, can be a good source of intelligence, and are often willing to provide recommendations.

Influencers

Connect with influencers such as consultants, bloggers, and speakers at conferences. If you mention something they have written or tell them you enjoyed their talk, many will be happy to connect.

Media

Editors, reporters, columnists, podcasters, bloggers, and freelance writers from your industry make great connections. Follow them first, then read and comment on their posts. Take your time and build the relationship. It can turn into coverage for your business down the road.

Associations

Association executives are usually extremely well-connected. Consider asking the executive director, subject matter experts, board members, and committee leaders to connect. As with influencers and the media, pay attention to what they are doing and support the organization.

How to Introduce Yourself

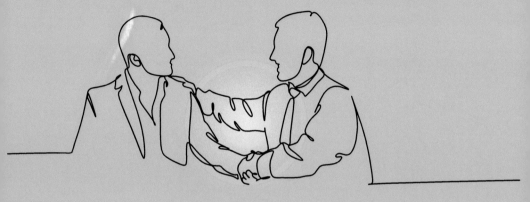

Even prospecting experts struggle to come up with an introduction strategy for LinkedIn that doesn't sound contrived.

We all have good intentions. However, our prospects don't know this when they get a LinkedIn message. They go on high alert ready to sniff out a sales message — and you know how they feel because you are on the receiving end of many sales messages too.

In fact, you probably get a ridiculous number of sales messages on LinkedIn. The increased use of bots and automation has created a real problem — one that has changed the advice we give to CEOs.

For years, we recommended personalizing connect requests.

But now, in many cases, a blank connect request will be more effective. It is seen as more authentic, especially for someone at the C-suite level. We now recommend that as your default.

However, if you have something meaningful to say, it is still a good idea to send a personal message.

Be relevant and honest. Show you are contacting them for a good reason.

You get 300 characters (35-50 words) for a standard connect request. InMails can be longer, but you still want to be concise. The recipient will only see the first 75 characters unless they click "More," so put the most important information at the beginning.

Note that you can now include an email address, phone number, or URL in your connect request.

It's important to know that if people feel that your connect request is too pushy, they can report you to LinkedIn. If they tell LinkedIn they don't know you, this is referred to as an IDK, meaning "I Don't Know." LinkedIn can limit your account if you receive as few as five IDKs.

Here are some strategies that currently work:

1. Reference a recent podcast.

Tell them what you enjoyed about it, in enough detail that they know you really listened.

2. Follow up on a profile visit.

If they viewed your profile and look relevant, a message like this works well:

"I notice that you viewed my profile. Were you looking for something specific? Maybe I can help you or point the way."

3. Congratulate them on a promotion or job change.

This provides an excellent opportunity to reach out, since people in a new role often look to buy new products or services.

"Congratulations on your promotion to VP of Enterprise Sales. Let me ask… if sales training is on your radar, could we have a call? We have a new training program that improves close rates by up to 37%."

4. Invite them to an event.

If you have an upcoming webinar or event at a conference, you can ask if they would like to join you.

How to Follow Up

If you sent a blank connect request, your best follow-up is none. Stay active on LinkedIn. Let them watch you and learn from you.

If you made an offer, promptly deliver what you promised.

You can also send a message offering to help if they ever need someone with your expertise.

Never assume that someone who accepted your connection is interested in buying from you and immediately start selling.

The most you should do is check in with them to see if they have one of the problems you can solve and invite them to have a conversation.

Think about LinkedIn as a place to build relationships over time, not the place you will make a quick sale.

Chapter 4

Building Relation- ships

Everyone pays attention to who is paying attention to them.

After your initial outreach, you want to build relationships with your new connections. Most will want to watch you and learn more about you and your business before they will be ready to engage. Others will be open to talking sooner. Either way, you want to stay active on LinkedIn so you keep your name in front of your connections and maintain mindshare.

How to Stay in Touch

Here are the easiest ways to stay in touch:

1. Congratulate!

LinkedIn notifies you when one of your connections is mentioned in the news, publishes a blog post, gets promoted, or changes jobs. (Note that someone who changes their headline can turn up in your news feed as a job change, so make sure their job has actually changed before you congratulate them.)

2. Engage with their content.

Check your news feed (on your home page) for status updates and blog posts published by your connections. When you like, comment on, or share those items, your connections know you are paying attention to them.

You can get notified as soon as they post if you go to their LinkedIn profile page and click on the bell icon to the right of their name. That will allow you to be one of the first to comment. And subsequent viewers have the opportunity to see your comment, so you get exposed to a wider audience.

3. Do a simple check-in.

There's value in sending a message to your connections from time to time, especially those you know well, to ask how things are going.

For those you do not know well, reach out and offer a free brainstorming session. Not everyone has time to do this, but people will remember that you offered to help, and it builds goodwill for the future. You might have some great conversations!

What to Post

Sharing interesting articles is an excellent way to maintain mindshare and add value to your network.

What type of information is most valued?

Content that is relevant to their job, such as:

- Breaking industry news

- Data

- New tools or services that could solve a common problem

- Tips about how to do something better

The more technical the information you share, the deeper your expertise is assumed to be. Don't shy away from highly technical articles if they're relevant for your connections.

When you share an article, add your insights:

- Why you found it useful

- Who else might find it interesting

- Quote from the article

- Share data cited in the article

Use hashtags to expand the audience for your posts (#ai or #DevSecOps, for example). And if the article is relevant to specific individuals, you can bring it to their attention by tagging them. Type the @ sign, then start typing their name. LinkedIn will suggest people with that name and you can select from that list. You do not have to be connected to someone to tag them.

There is no need to share a lot of articles — LinkedIn isn't Twitter! One per week is enough. If you are liking and commenting on your connections' posts, you will have plenty of activity in your account.

How to Get People to Engage with You

When you get people to engage with your update, your post becomes visible to their connections. This can vastly increase your reach. So how do you get people to engage?

Here are a few tips:

1. Engage with them.

The law of reciprocity applies to social media. If you consistently engage with someone's content, they are much more likely to engage with yours.

2. Make it easy.

Most people are on a mobile device and doing something else while they are on LinkedIn. Ask simple questions or conduct a poll. Make it easy, and they are more likely to do it.

3. Post about topics that matter.

People engage with posts that have meaning for them. When you talk about topics they care about, they are more likely to like and comment.

Chapter 5

Thought Leader-ship

LinkedIn is the ideal place to share your expertise.

When you are seen as a thought leader, more people are aware of you and your business, it is easier to get people to take meetings, you can charge higher prices, and you attract higher caliber employees.

Blogging

Every user on LinkedIn — even those with free accounts — can publish blog posts, which LinkedIn refers to as articles.

When you publish on LinkedIn and the people in your network interact with your post, it becomes visible to their networks. That immediately gives you higher readership than publishing on your website.

A blog post published on LinkedIn is available to search engines and will rank higher than the same post on your website, because LinkedIn has so much traffic that Google considers it an authority site.

Here are some tips for blogging on LinkedIn:

1. How often should you publish?

For most CEOs, one blog post a month is the ideal frequency. If that is too often for you, consider publishing quarterly. Your company may blog daily or weekly, but no one expects that frequency from an executive.

2. How long should a blog post be?

The ideal length is 500-1,000 words. There is data showing that longer posts are shared more often, but most people are reading on a mobile device and shorter content works better there. Don't worry about the length — make it as long or short as it needs to be to tell the story.

3. What should you write about?

Share your insights, vision, and perspective. Answer questions you are asked frequently. Tell stories — especially stories about your customers.

Video

Video gets 1,200% more engagement than other types of posts. LinkedIn is currently prioritizing video in the news feed, so your videos get more exposure than blog posts, articles, or updates. It's worth the effort to use videos to get your story out there.

Native videos (informal videos taken with a phone) are watched three times longer than professionally packaged videos. And they provide the easiest and least expensive way to get started with videos.

Use short videos to tell customer stories, share the excitement of live events, or offer bite-sized insights.

Here are some tips:

- Invest in quality lighting and a good microphone.

- Choose a simple but interesting backdrop.

- Keep your videos short, ideally under a minute.

- Add captions. 80% of the people on LinkedIn watch with the sound off.

Documents

You can upload a document as an update. Some people refer to this as a carousel, others as a mini-guide. It looks like a PowerPoint, with short and simple text on each page.

These posts are given priority in the news feed, in part because a multi-page document gets a long "dwell" time as people page through the document.

The most effective documents we see are extremely simple, with just a few words per page. However, you can upload case studies and ebooks.

Polls

Polls provide a fun way to engage with your network and get feedback. They also have good reach and can start interesting conversations.

Your poll question is limited to 140 characters, and you can only have 4 options of 30 characters each.

Chapter 6

LinkedIn Tips & Strategies

Tailor your activity on LinkedIn to accomplish your business goals.

So far, we have been sharing advice relevant for CEOs in general. Now, let's talk about what you can do on LinkedIn to advance specific business goals.

For all these strategies, there is a unifying theme: Tailor your profile and activity to attract the type of people you want to impress.

Demonstrate your expertise in the areas those people care about and build trust, so they are comfortable doing business with you.

Then stay active on LinkedIn so when an opportunity arises, you're the person they think of.

Lead Generation

LinkedIn is the perfect place to prospect if you sell to professionals or executives. You can identify ideal customers, introduce yourself, educate people, maintain mindshare, and build relationships.

LinkedIn is considered the best social network for B2B lead generation and is responsible for 80% of all B2B leads from social media.

Here are some tips to help you optimize your presence for brand awareness and lead generation:

Your profile

Write as if you are speaking to customers. Talk about who you help and how you help them.

Tell the story of your expertise, so people appreciate the value you bring to a sales conversation.

Share why what you do matters to you. As Simon Sinek says, people buy your "why" before they buy anything else.

Align your profile with your customers. Use industry-specific or technical language where appropriate. Allow customers to see that you are like them.

Your network

People who view your profile will be able to see what connections you have in common. Connect with influencers, association executives, consultants, editors, podcasters, and others who are respected in your industry.

Connect to clients, prospects, partners, and members of your team.

Your updates

Share company news and accomplishments, but don't only talk about your business.

Interact with thought leaders, partners, and customers.

Congratulate partners, customers, prospects, and influencers on their wins.

Your blogs/videos

Share your customer stories.

Explain your methodology, process, or technology.

Answer questions you are asked frequently.

Proactively address objections.

Provide insights into current trends in your industry.

Product Launches

When you're launching a new product, you are in the spotlight. Editors and reporters will go to your LinkedIn profile to get background information before interviewing you. Make sure your LinkedIn presence tells the story of your new product.

Your profile

> Add a paragraph about your new solution to your About section or current job description.

> Upload a datasheet, brochure, PowerPoint, or video that introduces the new product and provides details.

> Update your header graphic to include an image of the new product.

Your network

> Connect to influencers who are relevant to the new product. This might include prospects, industry experts, or the media.

> Connect to beta users and partners who are involved in the launch.

Your updates

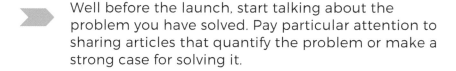 Well before the launch, start talking about the problem you have solved. Pay particular attention to sharing articles that quantify the problem or make a strong case for solving it.

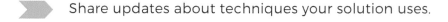 Share updates about techniques your solution uses.

 If you have new partners for this product, share their news. When they share information about your launch, make sure you like and share their posts.

Your blogs/videos

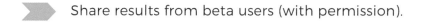 Talk about the problem you have solved — this is much more useful than talking about the solution, especially in the beginning. You want people to fully understand why this is a problem that was worth solving, why it is essential that they solve it, and why your solution is better than the other alternatives.

Share results from beta users (with permission).

Employer Branding

When you, your leadership team, and hiring managers have strong personal brands, you can attract higher caliber candidates and gain a competitive advantage in recruiting. Here are a few tips for using your personal brand to enhance recruiting:

Your profile

- Mention in your headline that you are hiring, or use the #Hiring photo frame. (You must have a current job posting on LinkedIn to use this frame.)

- Add gender pronouns to your profile.

- Record the correct pronunciation of your name.

- In your About section, talk about your company culture, your leadership philosophy, the type of people you want to hire, and who thrives in your organization.

- Upload photos and videos of your team.

- Ask for recommendations from people who work for you.

- Give recommendations to people who work for you, showing that you appreciate their work.

- If your company has received any "best places to work" awards, feature those on your profile.

- If your company volunteers as a team, include that in the Volunteer section.

Your network

> Connect with people who you would like to hire someday or who are respected by the type of people you want to hire.

> Connect with people who can make referrals: employees, colleagues, and peers.

Your updates

> Show your traction.

> Share blog posts that support your management style, philosophy, and culture.

> Share news that aligns you with the type of people you want to hire.

> Like and share updates from employees and peers.

Your blogs/videos

> Tell stories about your company culture, leadership style, and management philosophy.

> Talk about company values, such as work/life balance or education.

> Talk about diversity.

> Explain why you offer the benefits you do.

> Mention what's cool or unique about your company.

> Show your team talking about what they love about your company.

Board Role

Consider what you bring to an advisory board, non-profit board, or board of directors. What role can you fill? What knowledge and experience do you bring to the table? Package yourself and make sure your LinkedIn presence tells that story.

Being active on LinkedIn brings you to the attention of more people and helps you maintain mindshare with people in your network who can refer you. Here are some tips:

Your profile

> Showcase the expertise most relevant for a board.

> Incorporate a wide range of keywords.

> Use a header background photo from a conference or speaking engagement.

Your network

> Connect with other CEOs and board members.

> Consider connecting with executive recruiters who can make board recommendations.

Your updates

- Share blog posts and news relevant to the type of organization you want to serve.

- Demonstrate expertise in the industry and subject matter.

- Engage with peers and industry experts.

Your blogs/videos

- Cover topics that showcase your expertise and abilities.

- Discuss governance issues; show you understand the way boards think.

- Share your insights on business trends.

Fundraising

You can guarantee that anyone considering an investment in your business will look at your LinkedIn profile. To impress them, your profile should tell a compelling story of your vision, your expertise, and your traction.

Your profile

> Highlight your most impressive accomplishments (such as prior exits) in your headline and About section.

> Use your Featured section to showcase the most impressive articles about the business, your best podcast interviews, and announcements about funding and partnerships.

> Show how you obtained the experience that makes you uniquely qualified to deliver on your vision.

> Incorporate keywords related to the problem you solve, the type of solution you offer, and the industry you serve.

Your network

> Connect with CEOs of funded companies and other founders.

> Connect with thought leaders in your space and others who investors respect.

Your updates

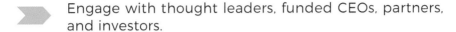 Engage with thought leaders, funded CEOs, partners, and investors.

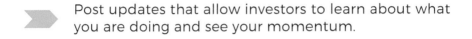 Post updates that allow investors to learn about what you are doing and see your momentum.

Your blogs/videos file

Tell stories about your customers and the results they have achieved.

Talk about the problems you solve, how important the problems are, and the consequences of not solving them.

Explain why your solution is superior to other ways of solving the problem.

Speakers

If you want more speaking engagements, use LinkedIn to become more findable, and make sure your profile includes video clips from speaking engagements that show how dynamic you are.

Your profile

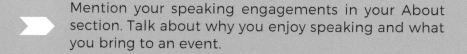

- Include "speaker" or "keynote speaker" in your headline.

- Mention your speaking engagements in your About section. Talk about why you enjoy speaking and what you bring to an event.

- Use a photo of you giving a keynote as your header graphic.

- Upload video clips from speaking engagements.

- Ask people who hired you or have heard you speak to give you recommendations.

- List public speaking and related topics as skills, and seek endorsements for those skills.

Your network

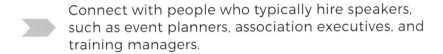 Connect with people who typically hire speakers, such as event planners, association executives, and training managers.

 Connect with other industry experts and speakers on this topic.

Your updates

Share news related to your areas of expertise.

Like and share blog posts from other experts.

Like and share news from organizations where you would like to speak.

Your blogs/videos

Share tips and advice in your areas of expertise.

Provide your unique viewpoint. The more you differentiate yourself, the easier it is to get speaking engagements.

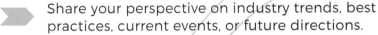 Share your perspective on industry trends, best practices, current events, or future directions.

Media Coverage

Do you want to be quoted in the press? Featured as a guest on the news or a talk show? Be on more podcasts? Use your LinkedIn presence to demonstrate subject matter expertise and show that you are media savvy.

Your profile

> Include keywords about your area of expertise in your headline and throughout your profile.

> Mention prior media coverage in your About section.

> Use a photo of you speaking as your header graphic.

> Use your Featured section to highlight video clips from TV appearances, podcasts, and articles.

Your network

> Connect with producers, podcasters, and bookers.

> Connect with other industry experts and speakers on this topic.

Your updates

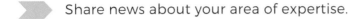

Share news about your area of expertise.

Like and share blog posts from other experts.

Like and share news from organizations where you would like to speak.

Your blogs/videos

Share insights in your areas of expertise.

Provide a clear and unique viewpoint. The more you differentiate yourself, the easier it is to get booked.

New CEO

When you start a new business, LinkedIn can be your secret weapon!

LinkedIn is the simplest and least expensive way to promote your new venture to the people most likely to become your new customers, partners, investors, and employees — the people already in your network. You want to maintain mindshare, educate them about the new business, and let them see your momentum.

Here are tips to optimize LinkedIn when you transition from employee to boss and start building momentum for your new venture:

Your profile

Rewrite your headline to include your new title, the problems you solve, and the people you help.

Use a header graphic that incorporates the new company logo and tagline,

Draft a new About section and tell people what you are doing in your new venture, why that matters to you, and why they should do business with you.

Add the new job to your Experience section.

Update previous job descriptions to show how you gained the expertise needed to achieve your current vision and why you will be successful.

Incorporate relevant keywords throughout your profile.

Evaluate the rest of your profile and add any elements that will establish credibility, show early traction, and demonstrate momentum.

Your network

▶ Use LinkedIn's search and filter features to find influencers and potential stakeholders in your new venture.

▶ Connect with and/or follow them.

▶ Click on the bell icon on their profile, so you'll get notifications when they are active on LinkedIn and can quickly comment on their posts.

Your updates

▶ Start posting about your new venture as soon as your profile is updated.

▶ If you are pre-MVP: Create posts that demonstrate your knowledge and insights in this area, the size and importance of the problem you are solving, the consequences of not solving it, and why your approach to solving it is better than the alternatives.

▶ As you grow: Shift your focus to traction, and tell stories about customer successes and the culture you are building.

▶ Be consistent and frequent in posting.

▶ Engage with the people who are already in your network.

▶ Engage with people who are respected by your stakeholders.

Exiting an Organization

When a CEO transitions from an organization, it can mean big changes for everyone — employees, the leadership team, customers, and partners. All those shareholders, plus analysts and the media, closely watch each step of the transition. You want to exit in a way that sets up a positive future for all parties.

LinkedIn offers transitioning CEOs a platform where their shareholders are already paying close attention to business. And, just as importantly, it lets you control the narrative and tell your story in your way.

Your profile

- Replace your corporate email address with a personal one.

- Remove links to the website and any other previous company info.

- Review and cull the Featured section, so it reflects your background and accomplishments versus those of the company.

- Review the Skills section to see if you need any updates to align with industry trends.

- When you set an end date, also post a thank you note for the people you worked with. Showcase highlights and accomplishments while you were there, and be generous with your parting words. Posts like this often generate thousands of views, likes, and comments, so be intentional and gracious.

- If you don't want to look unemployed, leave the Experience entry as "present" (up to nine months).

- Highlight advisory or board roles by dragging and dropping these entries above the previous job.

- Employ yourself — in your own company. Create a consulting company entry using "Your Name + Associates," and draft an elevator pitch — define your potential clients, the problems you solve, and why people should work with you.

Your network

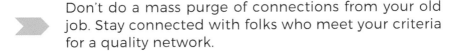 Don't do a mass purge of connections from your old job. Stay connected with folks who meet your criteria for a quality network.

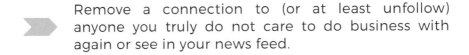 Remove a connection to (or at least unfollow) anyone you truly do not care to do business with again or see in your news feed.

Your updates

Don't stop communicating or go dark on social media. It's important that you engage and stay top of mind in your network.

Engage with the people in your network, especially your peers (other CEOs).

Like, comment, and participate in conversations on other people's posts. This engagement will have the biggest positive result for your investment of time.

Your blogs/videos

Share insights about current industry issues.

Stay positive, professional, and upbeat — always.

Job Search

Use LinkedIn to make yourself findable to executive recruiters. Craft your LinkedIn presence to tell the rich story of your expertise, build a large network, and stay active on LinkedIn so you maintain mindshare. Here are some tips for job seekers:

Your profile

▶ Share the full scope of your expertise, responsibilities, and accomplishments.

▶ Incorporate a wide range of keywords.

▶ Look at profiles of other CEOs to get ideas about how they present themselves.

Your network

▶ Connect with peers who can refer you.

▶ Connect with influencers in your industry.

▶ Connect with employees of companies you find interesting.

Your updates

▶ Share blog posts and news relevant to the type of job you want.

▶ Engage with other CEOs.

Your blogs/videos

▶ Discuss your leadership philosophy.

▶ Provide perspective on trends in the industry.

Taking a New Position

When you step into a new CEO job, almost everything is new and urgent. While it would be easy to delay updating your LinkedIn profile, don't put it off. The short time you invest to recalibrate your profile and presence to align with the new job and company will pay off in many ways, from saving time to building momentum.

Your profile

Change your headline to reflect your new position and how the company brings value. Time this change to correlate with the company announcement about you.

Use your background header to showcase the company name. If your company has templates for LinkedIn background headers, grab one for your profile. If they don't, ask your new team to create one.

Replace your personal (or old company) email address with your new company one.

Remove links to your previous employer's website and add links to the new one.

Revise your About section to reflect your vision for your new role — what you want to accomplish and why.

Check the tone of your profile and make sure you are writing to your new shareholders. What do they need to hear to begin to know, like, and trust you — to inspire them to go with you on this new journey?

Start filling the Featured section with links that align with and support your new role and company.

Your profile (continued)...

> Add the new job to your Experience section and link to the company's page on LinkedIn. Be sure to add a description — use this valuable space to let people know what you and the company are doing.

> Review the Skills section — do you need any updates to align with industry trends?

> Do a more comprehensive update, rethinking your entire Experience section for how your journey has uniquely qualified you for the new job.

Your network

> Connect with shareholders in the new company — leaders, partners, customers, and employees.

> Find, like, and comment on their posts.

> Connect with or follow industry thought leaders for the new company.

Your updates

 Share your vision.

Celebrate wins, milestones, and the people who make them happen.

Your blogs/videos

Post videos that articulate your vision, so shareholders get to know you better.

Share industry news and trends and your perspective on them.

Chapter 7

ChatGPT & LinkedIn

*ChatGPT makes building your brand
easier than you ever thought possible.*

AI writing tools, like ChatGPT, offer the potential to make it easier than ever to build a powerful CEO brand on LinkedIn. But it's not magic — you need to feed good information to the chatbot, generate multiple iterations of responses to refine the content, and do some final polishing of the writing. If you're willing to work at it a little, you can get some terrific results — quickly.

Even as I worked on this book, the AI landscape was changing daily, and I expect that to continue with more tools introduced and all of them becoming increasingly capable. Let's take a look at how you could use ChatGPT to help build your brand.

Enrich Your LinkedIn Profile

Headlines

ChatGPT is extremely good at generating all kinds of headlines, including headlines for your profile. Give it this information:

- Your title or role
- Your company name
- What industry you are in
- What type of customers you serve (or want more of)
- What kind of problems you solve
- What kind of results you achieve
- What accomplishments you are most proud of (such as exits)
- Where you are (if location matters)
- Someone else's headline that you like

Give ChatGPT a character limit — you could say "220 characters including spaces" or "120 characters" if you want a shorter version.

The first set of results is usually interesting but not what you need. Iterate to get some different versions you can play with. For example, you could say, "write to" and then describe your ideal customer. Or say, "inject humor" or "use more sophisticated language" or "use more technical language."

You could also give it a format to work with:

Please suggest 10 headlines based on the following format:
[title] at [company name] that helps [type of customers] solve [type of problem] and achieve [typical results] in [location], and who has achieved [accomplishments].

Once you have 20+ headlines to play with, mix and match the phrases to come up with your new headline.

Experience Section

ChatGPT can also help generate job descriptions for the Experience section of your profile. Cut and paste the details from your resume. Ask it for "a narrative entry for an Experience section on a LinkedIn profile. Maximum 2,000 characters, including spaces. Complete sentences and in past-tense verb form."

Repeat that process for every job description, and then edit the writing to make sure the output isn't too repetitive in style.

About Section

When you have a title and job description that you like, tell ChatGPT a little more about yourself. Why do you like your job or industry? What matters to you? What's unique about you or your company or team? Feed all of that, plus your title and job description, to ChatGPT. Ask it to "write an interesting About section for LinkedIn. Maximum 2,600 characters."

Don't settle for the first draft; get at least three or four versions. Ask ChatGPT to use the information to tell a story, speak to your ideal audience or a specific type of stakeholder, talk more about a specific aspect of your background, use more technical language, or make it funny.

With a variety of options to choose from, you can choose the phrasing you prefer and refine the narrative to get exactly what you want.

Brainstorm Content

ChatGPT is a deep well of blog and post topics. The more information and prompts that you feed it, the better topics it will deliver. Try these prompts:

- "As an expert in [your area of expertise], suggest 12 blog topics that will be fascinating to [your ideal client] who have [the problem you solve]."
- Ask ChatGPT what your ideal customer is worried about when they are in a specific situation. For example, "Acting as a B2B SaaS CEO who is preparing to raise their next round of financing, what worries are keeping you awake at night?"
- Describe your ideal customer and the type of solution you offer, then ask ChatGPT for the top questions that type of customer is likely to have about your solution.
- Ask for a list of reasons a type of customer would not buy your product or service. You can even ask how to handle those objections.

Draft Posts

When you have a topic — or a list of them — that will ring true with your audience, use ChatGPT to draft titles, hooks, body text, and calls to action for them.

As always with ChatGPT, you don't want to stop with the first set of responses. For titles, ask it to revise the list to:

- Make the titles more specific.
- Make the titles funnier.
- Use industry buzzwords.

Then move to the hook (you can ask specifically for hooks — ChatGPT knows what they are). Ask it to provide an opening sentence (or paragraph) that will draw people in and make them want to read the whole post. You can even ask for specific styles, like storytelling.

You can ask ChatGPT to outline a blog or post, and you can ask it to write the entire thing. Keep in mind that you will not get a draft that is 100% on point, accurate, and what you want. You'll need to check, edit, and refine. But, in our tests, ChatGPT delivered plenty of good ideas to work with — and it delivered them very quickly.

When you're ready for a call to action on your post, tell ChatGPT what you want the readers to do next (contact you, schedule a meeting, etc.) and ask it for a closing and call to action paragraph. You can specify the style (hard selling, no selling, helpful tone, encouraging tone, etc.), the action, and anything else you want to include.

Draft Comments

When you are sharing a company post or something you found interesting online, ask ChatGPT to draft text to introduce it. Copy and paste the text of the article, then specify what you want, including style and length. And then, of course, proof and edit the copy to make it your style. Voilà!

Pro Tip: ChatGPT works quickly — inputting your information will be the slowest part of using it. But remember, the chatbot only knows what has been fed into it by you and by other parties. Always fact-check what it gives you — dates, statistics, sources, quotations, everything — so you don't lose credibility with your audience.

About ProResource

ProResource is a marketing agency that specializes in executive branding — helping CEOs and leaders create their personal brands online, build their reputations as a thought leaders, and use social media to make faster progress on their business goals.

Founded in 2007, we have worked with more than 2,000 executives in businesses of all sizes, ranging from startups to Fortune 50 companies.

We help you use LinkedIn to:

- Build your personal brand as a leader.
- Get exposure for your company.
- Build a strong employer brand to gain a long-term competitive advantage in recruiting.
- Achieve your career goals.

Our services include:

- LinkedIn profile writing
- LinkedIn strategy
- Executive coaching
- Blog writing
- Account management

We can also provide LinkedIn training for your executives.

For more information, visit:
www.proresource.com

Please join us on a webinar or LinkedIn Live to get more tips and advice! For upcoming events, as well as archived Lives and webinars, visit:
www.proresource.com/webinars

ProResource, Inc.
8000 Towers Crescent Drive, Suite 1350
Vienna, VA 22182